Duncan Hines®

DELICIOUSLY
SIMPLE DESSERTS

Quick-to-Make Cakes

PETAL PINK ANGEL CAKE
12 to 16 servings

1 package Duncan Hines® Angel Food Cake Mix	1 teaspoon unflavored gelatin
¾ teaspoon almond extract, divided	¼ cup confectioners sugar
Red food coloring	¼ cup sliced natural almonds, for garnish
2 cups whipping cream, chilled	Fresh raspberries, for garnish

1. Preheat oven to 375°F.

2. Prepare cake batter following package directions. Fold in ½ teaspoon almond extract. Place 3 cups batter in medium bowl. Fold in 3 drops red food coloring. Spoon half the white batter into ungreased 10-inch tube pan. Cover with pink batter. Top with remaining white batter. Bake and cool cake following package directions.

3. Place whipping cream, gelatin and remaining ¼ teaspoon almond extract in large bowl. Beat at medium speed with electric mixer. Add confectioners sugar gradually. Beat at high speed until soft peaks form. Tint with 3 drops red food coloring.

4. To assemble, place cake on serving plate. Frost sides and top with whipped cream mixture. Decorate with sliced natural almonds and raspberries to form flowers (see Photo).

> **Tip:** *To prevent air pockets, use spatula to press batter into sides and bottom of pan.*

Petal Pink Angel Cake

CAPTIVATING CATERPILLAR CUPCAKES

24 cupcakes

1 package Duncan Hines® Moist
    Deluxe White Cake Mix
3 egg whites
1¼ cups water
    ⅓ cup Crisco® Oil or
        Crisco® Puritan® Oil
    ½ cup decorating star decors,
        divided
1 container (16 ounces) Duncan
    Hines® Vanilla Layer Cake
    Frosting

Green food coloring
6 chocolate sandwich cookies,
    finely crushed (see Tip)
    ½ cup candy-coated chocolate
        pieces
    ⅓ cup assorted jelly beans
    Assorted nonpareil decors

1. Preheat oven to 350°F. Place 24 (2½-inch) paper liners in muffin cups.

2. Combine cake mix, egg whites, water and oil in large bowl. Beat at low speed with electric mixer until moistened. Beat at medium speed for 2 minutes. Fold in ⅓ cup star decors. Fill paper liners about half full. Bake at 350°F for 18 to 23 minutes or until toothpick inserted in center comes out clean. Cool in pans 5 minutes. Remove to cooling racks. Cool completely.

3. Tint Vanilla frosting with green food coloring. Frost one cupcake. Sprinkle ½ teaspoon chocolate cookie crumbs on frosting. Arrange 4 candy-coated chocolate pieces to form caterpillar body. Place jelly bean at one end to form head. Attach remaining star and nonpareil decors with dots of frosting to form eyes. Repeat with remaining cupcakes.

Note: This recipe contains no cholesterol.

Tip: *To finely crush chocolate sandwich cookies, place cookies in a resealable plastic bag. Remove excess air from bag; seal. Press rolling pin on top of cookies to break into pieces. Continue pressing until evenly crushed.*

Captivating Caterpillar Cupcakes

BANANA STREUSEL SURPRISE   12 to 16 servings

1 package Duncan Hines® Moist
   Deluxe Banana Supreme
   Cake Mix
1 package (4-serving size) vanilla
   or banana cream instant
   pudding and pie filling mix
4 eggs
1 cup dairy sour cream

⅓ cup Crisco® Oil or
   Crisco® Puritan® Oil
½ cup chopped Fisher® pecans
   or walnuts
1 cup crushed chocolate-covered
   graham crackers
Confectioners sugar, for garnish

1. Preheat oven to 350°F. Grease and flour 10-inch Bundt® pan.

2. Combine cake mix, pudding mix, eggs, sour cream and oil in large bowl.
Beat at low speed with electric mixer until moistened. Beat at high speed for
2 minutes. Stir in pecans. Pour one-third of batter into pan. Sprinkle with half
the crushed graham crackers. Repeat layers, ending with batter. Bake at
350°F for 50 to 55 minutes or until toothpick inserted in center comes out
clean. Cool in pan 25 minutes. Invert onto serving plate. Dust with
confectioners sugar. Serve warm or cool completely.

> **Tip:** *For best results, bake cakes immediately after mixing the batter.*

SUZIE'S STRAWBERRY ANGEL DELIGHT   12 to 16 servings

1 package Duncan Hines® Angel
   Food Cake Mix
4 packages (3 ounces each)
   strawberry gelatin
3 cups boiling water
4 cups ice cubes

2 packages (10 ounces each)
   sweetened, frozen sliced
   strawberries, thawed
1 container (12 ounces) frozen
   whipped topping, thawed

(continued on page 8)

Banana Streusel Surprise

Suzie's Strawberry Angel Delight, continued

1. Preheat oven to 375°F.

2. Prepare, bake and cool cake following package directions. Trim crust from bottom of cake. Tear cake into bite-size pieces. Arrange in ungreased 13 × 9 × 2-inch pan.

3. Dissolve gelatin in large bowl with boiling water. Stir in ice and strawberries until mixture begins to thicken. Remove any remaining ice cubes. Pour gelatin mixture over cake pieces; stir gently. Spread with whipped topping. Refrigerate 2 hours or until ready to serve. Cut into squares.

> **Tip:** *For angel food cakes, always use a totally grease-free cake pan to get the best volume.*

CHOCOLATE CREAM TORTE   12 to 16 servings

1 package Duncan Hines® Moist
  Deluxe Devil's Food Cake Mix
1 package (8 ounces) cream
  cheese, softened
½ cup sugar
1 teaspoon vanilla extract

1 cup finely chopped Fisher®
  pecans
1 cup whipping cream, chilled
  Strawberry halves, for garnish
  Mint leaves, for garnish
  (optional)

1. Preheat oven to 350°F. Grease and flour two 8- or 9-inch round cake pans.

2. Prepare, bake and cool cake following package directions for basic recipe. Chill layers for ease in splitting.

3. Place cream cheese, sugar and vanilla extract in small bowl. Beat at low speed with electric mixer until smooth. Add pecans; stir until blended. Set aside. Beat whipping cream in small bowl until stiff peaks form. Fold whipped cream into cream cheese mixture.

4. To assemble, split each cake layer in half horizontally (see Tip). Place one cake layer on serving plate. Spread top with one-fourth of filling. Repeat with remaining layers and filling. Garnish with strawberry halves and mint leaves, if desired. Refrigerate until ready to serve.

> **Tip:** *To split layers evenly, measure cake with ruler. Divide into 2 equal layers. Mark with toothpicks. Cut through layers with serrated knife using toothpicks as guide.*

LEMON CHIFFON CAKE

12 to 16 servings

CAKE
1 package Duncan Hines® Angel
    Food Cake Mix
1 cup water
3 eggs
¾ cup Crisco® Oil or
    Crisco® Puritan® Oil

¼ cup all-purpose flour
1 tablespoon grated lemon peel
½ teaspoon vanilla extract

FROSTING
1 container (16 ounces) Duncan
    Hines® Vanilla Layer Cake
    Frosting
2 teaspoons butter or margarine,
    melted

2 teaspoons grated lemon peel
    Lemon slices, for
      garnish
    Mint leaves, for garnish
      (optional)

1. Preheat oven to 350°F.

2. **For cake,** combine Egg White Mixture (blue "A" packet) from Mix and water in large bowl. Beat at low speed with electric mixer for 1 minute. Beat at high speed for 5 to 10 minutes or until stiff peaks form; set aside.

3. Combine Cake Flour Mixture (red "B" packet) from Mix, eggs, oil, flour, 1 tablespoon lemon peel and vanilla extract in large bowl. Beat at low speed until blended. Beat at medium speed for 3 minutes. Fold in reserved beaten egg white mixture. Pour into ungreased 10-inch tube pan. Run knife through batter to remove air bubbles. Bake at 350°F for 45 to 55 minutes or until toothpick inserted in center comes out clean. Cool following package directions.

4. **For frosting,** combine Vanilla frosting, melted butter and 2 teaspoons lemon peel in medium bowl. Stir until thoroughly blended. Frost sides and top of cake. Garnish with lemon slices and mint leaves, if desired.

Tip: *Freeze extra grated lemon peel for future use.*

LUSCIOUS KEY LIME CAKE

12 to 16 servings

CAKE

1 package Duncan Hines® Moist Deluxe Lemon Supreme Cake Mix

1 package (4-serving size) lemon instant pudding and pie filling mix

4 eggs

1 cup Crisco® Oil or Crisco® Puritan® Oil

¾ cup water

¼ cup Key lime juice (see Tip)

GLAZE

2 cups confectioners sugar

⅓ cup Key lime juice

2 tablespoons water

2 tablespoons butter or margarine, melted

Additional confectioners sugar

Lime slices, for garnish

Fresh strawberry slices, for garnish (optional)

1. Preheat oven to 350°F. Grease and flour 10-inch Bundt® pan.

2. **For cake,** combine cake mix, pudding mix, eggs, oil, ¾ cup water and ¼ cup Key lime juice in large bowl. Beat at low speed with electric mixer until moistened. Beat at medium speed for 2 minutes. Pour into pan. Bake at 350°F for 50 to 60 minutes or until toothpick inserted in center comes out clean. Cool in pan 25 minutes. Invert onto cooling rack. Return cake to pan. Poke holes in top of warm cake with toothpick or long-tined fork.

3. **For glaze,** combine 2 cups confectioners sugar, ⅓ cup Key lime juice, 2 tablespoons water and melted butter in medium bowl. Pour slowly over top of warm cake. Cool completely. Invert onto serving plate. Dust with additional confectioners sugar. Garnish with lime slices and strawberry slices, if desired.

Tip: *Fresh or bottled lime juice may be substituted for the Key lime juice.*

Luscious Key Lime Cake

STRAWBERRY SUPREME

12 to 16 servings

1 package Duncan Hines® Moist
    Deluxe Strawberry Supreme
    Cake Mix
1 package (6-serving size) vanilla
    instant pudding and pie
    filling mix

3 cups milk
1 quart fresh strawberries, whole
    or sliced
1 bag (16 ounces) strawberry glaze
1 container (8 ounces) frozen
    whipped topping, thawed

1. Preheat oven to 350°F. Grease two Duncan Hines® Tiara Dessert Pans or
10½ × 1½-inch flan pans (see Tip).

2. Prepare cake following package directions for basic recipe. Divide evenly
into pans. Bake at 350°F for 28 to 31 minutes or until toothpick inserted in
center comes out clean. Cool in pans 10 minutes. Invert onto cooling racks.
Cool completely.

3. Prepare pudding following package directions using 3 cups milk. Spread
half the pudding into well of each cake.

4. Combine strawberries and glaze. Spoon half the strawberry mixture over
each pudding layer. Refrigerate until ready to serve. Garnish with whipped
topping just before serving.

> **Tip:** *When only one Tiara Dessert Pan is available, reserve half the cake
> batter. Cover and refrigerate until the first cake is baked.*

COCONUT CREAM CAKE

12 to 16 servings

CAKE

1 package Duncan Hines® Moist
    Deluxe White Cake Mix
1 package (4-serving size) coconut
    cream instant pudding and
    pie filling mix

4 eggs
1 cup water
⅓ cup Crisco® Oil or
    Crisco® Puritan® Oil
⅓ cup flaked coconut

FROSTING

2 cups whipping cream, chilled
¼ cup confectioners sugar

¼ cup dairy sour cream
2½ cups flaked coconut, divided

1. Preheat oven to 350°F. Grease and flour two 9-inch round cake pans.

2. **For cake,** combine cake mix, pudding mix, eggs, water and oil in large bowl. Beat at low speed with electric mixer until moistened. Beat at medium speed for 2 minutes. Stir in ⅓ cup coconut. Divide evenly into pans. Bake at 350°F for 32 to 37 minutes or until toothpick inserted in center comes out clean. Cool following package directions.

3. **For frosting,** place whipping cream in another large bowl. Beat at high speed until soft peaks form. Add confectioners sugar and sour cream. Beat until stiff peaks form. Fold in 1½ cups coconut. Fill and frost cake. Sprinkle with remaining 1 cup coconut. Refrigerate until ready to serve.

> **Tip:** *Before frosting any cake, let it cool completely. Never frost a warm cake unless the recipe directs you to do so.*

ALMOND POUND CAKE
12 to 16 servings

1 package Duncan Hines® Moist Deluxe White Cake Mix
1 package (4-serving size) vanilla instant pudding and pie filling mix
4 eggs
1 cup water
⅓ cup Crisco® Oil or Crisco® Puritan® Oil
1 tablespoon almond extract
¾ cup sliced Fisher® almonds, toasted and chopped (see Tip)
Confectioners sugar, for garnish

1. Preheat oven to 350°F. Grease and flour 10-inch Bundt® pan.

2. Combine cake mix, pudding mix, eggs, water, oil and almond extract in large bowl. Beat at low speed with electric mixer until moistened. Beat at medium speed for 2 minutes. Stir in almonds. Pour into pan. Bake at 350°F for 40 to 45 minutes or until toothpick inserted in center comes out clean. Cool in pan 25 minutes. Invert onto cooling rack. Cool completely. Dust with confectioners sugar.

> **Tip:** *To toast almonds, spread in single layer on baking sheet. Toast in 350°F oven for 4 to 6 minutes or until fragrant. Cool completely; chop.*

EASY CHOCOLATE
MINT CAKE

12 to 16 servings

2 packages (4 ounces each) sweet
  chocolate baking bars, chopped
1 package Duncan Hines® Moist
  Deluxe Fudge Marble Cake Mix
3 eggs
1¼ cups water
⅔ cup Crisco® Oil or
  Crisco® Puritan® Oil

1 teaspoon peppermint extract
¼ cup unsweetened cocoa
½ cup butter or margarine,
  softened
Mint leaves, for garnish
  (optional)

1. Preheat oven to 350°F. Grease and flour 10-inch Bundt® pan.

2. Place chocolate in 2-cup glass liquid measuring cup. Microwave at
MEDIUM (50% power) for 2 minutes. Stir; microwave 1 minute longer. Stir
until smooth. Cool while preparing cake.

3. Combine cake mix, eggs, water, oil and peppermint extract in large bowl.
Beat at low speed with electric mixer until moistened. Beat at medium speed
for 2 minutes. Combine 2½ cups cake batter, contents of cocoa packet from
Mix and unsweetened cocoa in medium bowl. Beat on low speed for 1 minute.
Pour batter without cocoa into pan. Spoon cocoa batter over center of batter in
pan. Bake at 350°F for 35 minutes or until toothpick inserted in center comes
out clean. Cool in pan 25 minutes. Invert onto cooling rack. Cool completely.

4. Add butter to cooled chocolate. Stir until smooth and thickened. Spoon
frosting over top of cake. Garnish with mint leaves, if desired.

Tip: *If 10-inch Bundt® pan is not available, a 10-inch tube pan may be used.*

Easy Chocolate Mint Cake

CHANTILLY CARROT CAKE   12 to 16 servings

CAKE

1 package Duncan Hines® Moist
Deluxe French Vanilla Cake Mix
1 package (4-serving size) vanilla
instant pudding and pie
filling mix

4 eggs
1 cup water
⅓ cup Crisco® Oil or
Crisco® Puritan® Oil
2 cups grated fresh carrots

FROSTING

1 can (15¼ ounces) crushed
pineapple, undrained
1 package (6-serving size) vanilla
instant pudding and pie
filling mix
½ cup chopped Fisher® pecans

1 container (12 ounces) frozen
whipped topping, thawed
Pineapple tidbits, for garnish
Mint leaves, for garnish
(optional)

1. Preheat oven to 350°F. Grease and flour three 9-inch round cake pans.

2. **For cake,** combine cake mix, 4-serving size pudding mix, eggs, water and oil in large bowl. Beat at low speed with electric mixer until moistened. Beat at medium speed for 2 minutes. Fold carrots into batter. Divide evenly into pans. Bake at 350°F for 25 to 30 minutes or until toothpick inserted in center comes out clean. Cool in pans 15 minutes. Invert onto cooling racks. Cool completely.

3. **For frosting,** combine crushed pineapple, 6-serving size pudding mix and pecans in large bowl. Fold in whipped topping. Place one cake layer on serving plate. Spread with one-fourth of frosting (about 1½ cups). Repeat layering two more times. Frost sides with remaining frosting. Garnish with pineapple tidbits and mint leaves, if desired. Refrigerate until ready to serve.

> **Tip:** *To keep the cake plate neat, place four pieces of waxed paper under edges of the bottom layer. After frosting, carefully slide out waxed paper.*

HOT FUDGE UPSIDE-DOWN CAKE

12 to 16 servings

FROSTING
- 1 package (6 ounces) semi-sweet chocolate chips
- ¾ cup firmly packed brown sugar
- ½ cup butter or margarine
- 3 tablespoons milk

CAKE
- 1 package Duncan Hines® Moist Deluxe White Cake Mix
- 3 egg whites
- 1¼ cups water
- ⅓ cup Crisco® Oil or Crisco® Puritan® Oil
- ½ cup chopped Fisher® pecans, for garnish (see Tip)

1. Preheat oven to 350°F. Grease 13 × 9 × 2-inch pan.

2. **For frosting,** combine chocolate chips, brown sugar, butter and milk in small saucepan. Heat on low heat, stirring until smooth. Pour into pan; spread evenly.

3. **For cake,** combine cake mix, egg whites, water and oil in large bowl. Beat at low speed with electric mixer until moistened. Beat at medium speed for 2 minutes. Pour over chocolate mixture in pan. Bake at 350°F for 35 to 40 minutes or until toothpick inserted in center comes out clean. Cool in pan 15 minutes. Invert onto serving platter or tray. Spread any remaining chocolate in pan on cake. Sprinkle with pecans. Serve warm.

> **Tip:** *For a delicious variation, garnish with ¼ cup flaked coconut in place of the pecans.*

Hot Fudge Upside-Down Cake

STRAWBERRY CELEBRATION CAKE

12 to 16 servings

1 package Duncan Hines® Moist
    Deluxe Strawberry Supreme
    Cake Mix

1 cup strawberry preserves,
    heated

FROSTING
2 packages (3 ounces each)
    cream cheese, softened
½ cup butter or margarine,
    softened

1½ teaspoons vanilla extract
4 cups confectioners sugar
    Strawberry halves, for garnish
    Mint leaves, for garnish

1. Preheat oven to 350°F. Grease and flour 10-inch Bundt® pan.

2. Prepare, bake and cool cake following package directions for basic recipe.

3. Split cake horizontally into three even layers. Place bottom cake layer on serving plate. Spread with ½ cup warm preserves. Repeat layering. Top with remaining cake layer.

4. **For frosting,** combine cream cheese, butter and vanilla extract in large bowl. Beat at low speed with electric mixer until smooth and creamy. Add confectioners sugar, ½ cup at a time, beating until smooth. Frost cake. Garnish with strawberry halves and mint leaves. Refrigerate until ready to serve.

> **Tip:** *For a quick and easy frosting, use 1 container (16 ounces) Duncan Hines® Cream Cheese Layer Cake Frosting.*

Strawberry Celebration Cake

GERMAN CHOCOLATE CAKE   12 to 16 servings

CAKE

1 package (4 ounces) sweet
  chocolate baking bar, chopped
½ cup boiling water
1 package Duncan Hines® Moist
  Deluxe White Cake Mix

3 eggs
¼ cup butter or margarine,
  softened

FROSTING

⅔ cup sugar
⅔ cup evaporated milk
2 egg yolks
⅓ cup butter or margarine
1⅓ cups flaked coconut

1 cup chopped Fisher® pecans
½ teaspoon vanilla extract
1 container (16 ounces) Duncan
  Hines® Chocolate Layer
  Cake Frosting

1. Preheat oven to 350°F. Grease and flour two 9-inch round cake pans.

2. **For cake,** place chocolate in 2-cup glass measuring cup. Add ½ cup boiling water. Stir until chocolate is melted. Add additional water to equal 1¼ cups liquid. Combine cake mix, eggs, chocolate liquid mixture and ¼ cup butter in large bowl. Beat at low speed with electric mixer until moistened. Beat at medium speed for 2 minutes. Divide evenly into pans. Bake at 350°F for 27 to 32 minutes or until toothpick inserted in center comes out clean. Cool following package directions.

3. **For frosting,** combine sugar, evaporated milk, egg yolks and ⅓ cup butter in medium saucepan. Cook on medium heat, stirring constantly, until mixture comes to a boil. Remove from heat. Add coconut, pecans and vanilla extract. Stir until thick. Cool 15 minutes.

4. To assemble, place one cake layer on serving plate. Spread with half the coconut frosting. Top with second cake layer. Spread Chocolate frosting on sides of cake. Spread remaining coconut frosting on top of cake.

> **Tip:** *Store leftover Chocolate frosting tightly covered in refrigerator. Spread frosting between graham crackers for a quick snack.*

German Chocolate Cake

DAZZLING RAINBOW CAKE   12 to 16 servings

1 package Duncan Hines® Moist
    Deluxe Cake Mix (any flavor)
3 eggs, beaten lightly
1⅓ cups water
⅓ cup Crisco® Oil or
    Crisco® Puritan® Oil
1 container (16 ounces) Duncan
    Hines® Vanilla Layer Cake
    Frosting

1 package (24 ounces) assorted
    small gumdrops
1 teaspoon water
6 drops green food coloring
½ cup flaked coconut

1. Preheat oven to 350°F. Grease 13 × 9 × 2-inch pan.

2. Place cake mix, beaten eggs, 1⅓ cups water and oil in pan. Stir with fork until moist and well blended. Spread evenly in pan. Bake at 350°F for 35 to 38 minutes or until toothpick inserted in center comes out clean. Cool completely.

3. Spread Vanilla frosting on top of cake. Draw outline of rainbow in frosting with tip of knife. Separate gumdrops according to colors. Place gumdrops in rows according to colors on frosting following outline for rainbow (see Photo).

4. Place 1 teaspoon water and green food coloring in jar or container with tight fitting lid; shake to mix. Add coconut; shake until evenly tinted. Sprinkle coconut under rainbow for grass.

Tip: *Since an electric mixer is not required, this is a great cake for children to help prepare. Be sure to blend batter well so there isn't any dry mix left. Spread batter evenly into all the corners of the pan with the fork. Don't worry if there are a few lumps in the batter.*

Dazzling Rainbow Cake

RAISIN CINNAMON BREAD

2 loaves

BREAD

1 package Duncan Hines® Bakery Style Cinnamon Swirl Muffin Mix

2 cups all-purpose flour

1 package (¼ ounce) quick-rise yeast

1 cup hot water (see Tip)

¼ cup butter or margarine, melted and divided

1 egg, slightly beaten

1 cup raisins

FROSTING

1 cup confectioners sugar

1 tablespoon butter or margarine, melted

3½ teaspoons milk

1. **For bread,** combine muffin mix, flour and yeast in large bowl. Stir until well blended. Stir in hot water and 2 tablespoons melted butter. Stir in egg. Cover and let rise for 1 hour or until doubled. Punch down. Invert onto floured surface. Cover with inverted bowl. Let rest for 10 minutes.

2. Preheat oven to 375°F. Grease two 8½ × 4½ × 2½-inch loaf pans.

3. Divide dough in half. Roll half the dough into 12 × 7-inch rectangle. Brush with 1 tablespoon melted butter. Knead swirl packet from Mix. Spread contents of half the packet over butter. Combine contents of topping packet from Mix and raisins. Sprinkle half the raisin mixture over dough. Starting at short end, roll up dough jelly-roll fashion. Place in greased loaf pan. Repeat with remaining dough and filling. Bake at 375°F for 30 to 35 minutes or until golden brown. Cool in pans 5 minutes. Remove to cooling racks and cool completely.

4. **For frosting,** combine confectioners sugar, 1 tablespoon melted butter and milk in small bowl. Stir until thick and creamy. Frost top of each loaf with half the frosting.

> **Tip:** *For best results, make sure water is between 120° and 130°F before adding to flour mixture.*

Raisin Cinnamon Bread

4TH OF JULY DESSERT MUFFINS

12 muffins

1 package Duncan Hines® Bakery Style Blueberry Muffin Mix	1½ tablespoons strawberry jam
1 egg	Red food coloring
¾ cup milk	½ cup chopped Fisher® pecans, divided

1. Preheat oven to 400°F. Place 12 (2½-inch) paper liners in muffin cups.

2. Rinse blueberries from Mix with cold water and drain.

3. Empty muffin mix in medium bowl. Break up any lumps. Add egg and milk. Stir until moistened, about 50 strokes. Pour one-third of batter into small bowl. Stir in jam, 4 drops food coloring and ¼ cup pecans. Fold blueberries into remaining batter; place 1 heaping teaspoon in each cup, spreading evenly. Spoon 1 heaping teaspoon strawberry batter on blueberry layer, spreading evenly. Divide remaining blueberry batter over strawberry batter, spreading evenly. Sprinkle tops with remaining ¼ cup pecans and contents of topping packet from Mix. Bake at 400°F for 18 to 23 minutes or until toothpick inserted in center comes out clean. Cool in pan 5 to 10 minutes. Serve warm or cool completely on cooling racks.

> **Tip:** *For a delicious no-cholesterol variation, substitute 2 egg whites for the whole egg and ¾ cup water for the milk.*

BLUEBERRY COFFEECAKE

9 servings

COFFEECAKE

1 package Duncan Hines® Blueberry Muffin Mix	½ cup orange juice
2 egg whites	½ cup strawberry preserves

CRUMB TOPPING

½ cup chopped Fisher® pecans	2 tablespoons margarine, softened
¼ cup firmly packed brown sugar	1 tablespoon all-purpose flour

(continued on page 32)

Blueberry Coffeecake, continued

1. Preheat oven to 350°F. Grease 8-inch square pan.

2. Rinse blueberries from Mix with cold water and drain.

3. **For coffeecake,** place muffin mix in medium bowl. Break up any lumps. Add egg whites and orange juice. Stir until moistened, about 50 strokes. Fold in blueberries. Spread in pan. Top with strawberry preserves.

4. **For crumb topping,** combine pecans, brown sugar, margarine and flour. Stir until mixture is crumbly. Sprinkle evenly on batter. Bake at 350°F for 35 to 40 minutes or until toothpick inserted in center comes out clean. Serve warm or cool completely.

Note: This recipe contains no cholesterol.

Tip: *To keep blueberries from discoloring batter, drain on paper towels after rinsing.*

BREAKFAST SHORTCAKE   8 servings

1 package Duncan Hines®
  Blueberry Muffin Mix
½ teaspoon baking powder
1 egg
1½ cups vanilla yogurt, divided
1 tablespoon lemon juice

1 teaspoon grated lemon peel
Assorted fruit pieces such as
  strawberry slices, pineapple
  tidbits, grape halves, peach or
  nectarine slices

1. Preheat oven to 400°F. Grease 9-inch round cake pan.

2. Combine muffin mix and baking powder in large bowl. Break up any lumps. Add egg, ½ cup yogurt, lemon juice and lemon peel. Stir until moistened, about 50 strokes. Pour into pan. Bake at 400°F for 14 to 16 minutes or until toothpick inserted in center comes out clean. Cool in pan 5 minutes. Invert onto cooling rack. Turn right-side up.

3. Rinse blueberries from Mix with cold water and drain. Add assorted fruit pieces. Toss gently to mix. To serve, cut warm shortcake into 8 wedges. Spoon 2 tablespoons remaining yogurt over each wedge. Top with fruit mixture.

Tip: *For an easy flavor variation, substitute 1 tablespoon orange juice for the lemon juice and 1 teaspoon grated orange peel for the lemon peel.*

Breakfast Shortcake

CHERRY CROWN DANISH   3 coffeecakes

COFFEECAKES

1 package Duncan Hines® Moist
   Deluxe Yellow Cake Mix
5 cups all-purpose flour
2 packages (¼ ounce each)
   quick-rise yeast

2½ cups hot water (120° to 130°F)
¼ cup plus 3 tablespoons butter or
   margarine, melted and divided
1 egg, slightly beaten

FILLING

2 cans (16 ounces each) red tart
   cherries packed in water
⅓ cup firmly packed brown sugar
⅓ cup granulated sugar
¼ cup cornstarch

½ teaspoon ground cinnamon
1½ tablespoons butter or margarine
1 teaspoon vanilla extract
1 teaspoon almond extract

TOPPING

1 package (3 ounces) cream cheese,
   softened
¾ cup confectioners sugar

1½ teaspoons milk
½ teaspoon vanilla extract

1. **For coffeecakes,** combine cake mix, flour and yeast in large bowl. Stir until
well blended. Stir in hot water and ¼ cup melted butter. Stir in egg. Cover and
let rise 1 hour or until doubled. Punch down. Invert onto well-floured surface.
Cover with inverted bowl. Let rest for 10 minutes.

2. Preheat oven to 375°F. Grease three 9-inch round cake pans.

3. **For filling,** drain cherries, reserving 1 cup juice; set aside. Combine brown
sugar, granulated sugar, cornstarch and cinnamon in large saucepan. Stir in
reserved 1 cup juice. Cook and stir on medium heat until mixture is thick and
bubbly. Boil for 1 minute, stirring constantly. Add cherries; cook for 1 minute
or until mixture comes to a boil. Remove from heat. Stir in 1½ tablespoons
butter, 1 teaspoon vanilla extract and almond extract; set aside.

4. Knead dough 8 to 10 times on well-floured surface. Divide into thirds.
Place dough in greased pans, stretching to cover bottom evenly. Spoon one-
third of cherry filling in center of each dough, spreading to within 1 inch of
dough edge. Bake at 375°F for 30 to 35 minutes or until deep golden brown.
Brush edges with remaining 3 tablespoons melted butter. Cool in pans
5 minutes. Loosen edges with knife and remove to cooling racks.

5. **For topping,** combine all topping ingredients in medium bowl. Beat until
smooth and creamy. Drizzle over cooled coffeecakes.

Tip: *For best results, allow yeast dough to rise in a warm, draft-free place.*

ORANGE ZUCCHINI LOAVES   2 loaves (24 slices)

LOAVES
1 package Duncan Hines® Orange
   Supreme Cake Mix
3 egg whites
¾ cup water
⅓ cup Crisco® Oil or
   Crisco® Puritan® Oil

1 teaspoon ground cinnamon
1 cup grated zucchini
2 teaspoons grated orange peel
   (see Tip)

SYRUP
¼ cup granulated sugar
2 tablespoons orange juice
   Confectioners sugar, for garnish

Orange slices, for garnish
   (optional)

1. Preheat oven to 350°F. Grease and flour two 8½ × 4½ × 2½-inch loaf pans.

2. **For loaves,** combine cake mix, egg whites, water, oil and cinnamon in large bowl. Beat at low speed with electric mixer until moistened. Beat at medium speed for 2 minutes. Fold in zucchini and orange peel. Divide evenly into pans. Bake at 350°F for 50 to 55 minutes or until toothpick inserted in center comes out clean. Cool in pans 15 minutes. Loosen loaves from pans. Invert onto cooling racks. Turn right-side up. Poke holes in tops of warm loaves with toothpick or long-tined fork.

3. **For syrup,** combine granulated sugar and orange juice in small saucepan. Cook on medium heat, stirring constantly, until sugar dissolves. Spoon hot syrup evenly over each loaf. Cool completely. Garnish with confectioners sugar and orange slices, if desired.

Note: This recipe contains no cholesterol.

Tip: *When grating orange peel, avoid bitter white portion known as the pith.*

DANISH TURBAN COFFEECAKES

3 coffeecakes

COFFEECAKES
1 package Duncan Hines® Moist
   Deluxe Yellow Cake Mix
5 cups all-purpose flour
2 packages (¼ ounce each)
   quick-rise yeast

2½ cups hot water (120° to 130°F)
¼ cup plus 3 tablespoons butter
   or margarine, melted and
   divided
1 egg, slightly beaten

STREUSEL FILLING
¾ cup firmly packed brown sugar
½ cup chopped Fisher® pecans

2 tablespoons all-purpose flour
2 teaspoons ground cinnamon

TOPPING
1½ cups confectioners sugar
2½ tablespoons milk

1 teaspoon vanilla extract

1. **For coffeecakes,** combine cake mix, 5 cups flour and yeast in large bowl. Stir until well blended. Stir in hot water and ¼ cup melted butter. Stir in egg. Cover; let rise for 1 hour or until doubled. Punch down. Invert onto well-floured surface. Cover with inverted bowl. Let rest for 10 minutes.

2. Preheat oven to 375°F. Grease 3 large baking sheets.

3. **For streusel filling,** combine brown sugar, pecans, 2 tablespoons flour and cinnamon in medium bowl; set aside.

4. Knead dough 8 to 10 times on well-floured surface. Divide into thirds. Roll one-third of dough into 14 × 6-inch rectangle. Brush with 1 tablespoon melted butter. Sprinkle ½ cup filling over dough. Starting at long end, roll up dough jelly-roll fashion. Connect ends to form ring. Place on greased baking sheet. Cut eight ½-inch-deep slits in top of coffeecake. Repeat with remaining dough and filling. Bake at 375°F for 22 to 27 minutes or until golden brown. Remove to cooling racks.

5. **For topping,** combine confectioners sugar, milk and vanilla extract in small bowl. Stir until smooth. Drizzle over warm coffeecakes. Serve warm or cool completely.

> **Tip:** *For a delicious flavor variation, substitute 1 can (21 ounces) blueberry pie filling for the streusel filling.*

Danish Turban Coffeecake

SUNSHINE MUFFIN TOPS

23 muffin tops

MUFFIN TOPS

1 package Duncan Hines® Bakery
  Style Cinnamon Swirl
  Muffin Mix
½ cup all-purpose flour
1 teaspoon baking powder
1 cup orange juice
1 egg

1 tablespoon Crisco® Oil or
  Crisco® Puritan® Oil
1 cup fresh peaches, sliced and
  chopped (see Tip)
¾ cup chopped Fisher® pecans
½ cup golden raisins

GLAZE

½ cup confectioners sugar
2½ teaspoons water

¼ cup chopped Fisher® pecans

1. Preheat oven to 375°F. Grease baking sheets.

2. **For muffin tops,** combine muffin mix, contents of topping packet from Mix, flour and baking powder in large bowl. Break up any lumps. Knead swirl packet from Mix for 10 seconds before opening. Cut off one end of swirl packet. Squeeze contents onto dry ingredients. Add orange juice, egg and oil. Stir until thoroughly blended, about 50 strokes. Fold in peaches, ¾ cup pecans and raisins. Drop by level ¼ measuring cupfuls 2 inches apart onto greased baking sheets. Bake at 375°F for 14 to 16 minutes or until set. Remove immediately to cooling racks.

3. **For glaze,** combine confectioners sugar and water in small bowl. Stir until smooth. Drizzle over warm muffin tops. Sprinkle with ¼ cup pecans. Serve warm or cool completely.

Tip: *Frozen peach slices, thawed and chopped, may be substituted for fresh peaches.*

Sunshine Muffin Tops

AHA! BLUEBERRY QUICK BREAD

1 loaf (12 slices)

1 package Duncan Hines® Bakery
Style Blueberry Muffin Mix

⅓ cup Fisher® sliced almonds

FILLING

1 package (8 ounces) cream cheese,
softened
1 egg
⅓ cup sugar

1 tablespoon all-purpose flour
1 tablespoon grated lemon peel,
divided

1. Preheat oven to 350°F. Grease and flour 9 × 5 × 3-inch loaf pan.

2. Rinse blueberries from Mix with cold water and drain. Combine contents of topping packet from Mix with almonds; set aside.

3. **For filling,** combine cream cheese, egg, sugar, flour and 1 teaspoon lemon peel in small bowl. Beat at low speed with electric mixer until smooth; set aside.

4. Prepare muffin mix following package directions. Fold in blueberries and remaining 2 teaspoons lemon peel. Pour two-thirds of batter into pan. Spoon filling evenly over batter. Add remaining batter. Sprinkle with almond mixture. Bake at 350°F for about 1 hour or until toothpick inserted in center comes out clean. Cool in pan 10 minutes. Loosen loaf from pan. Invert onto cooling rack. Turn right-side up. Cool completely.

Tip: *To help keep topping intact when removing loaf from pan, place aluminum foil on top.*

ORANGE PECAN BRUNCH CAKE

12 to 16 servings

1 package Duncan Hines® Moist
Deluxe Orange Supreme
Cake Mix
3 eggs
⅔ cup dairy sour cream
½ cup water
⅓ cup Crisco® Oil or
Crisco® Puritan® Oil
⅓ cup chopped Fisher® pecans

2 tablespoons lemon juice
1 teaspoon ground cinnamon
Mandarin orange segments
Strawberry slices
Kiwifruit slices
½ cup apricot preserves,
heated and strained
Mint leaves, for garnish
(optional)

1. Preheat oven to 350°F. Grease and flour 10-inch Bundt® or tube pan.

2. Combine cake mix, eggs, sour cream, water, oil, pecans, lemon juice and cinnamon in large bowl. Beat at low speed with electric mixer until moistened. Beat at medium speed for 2 minutes. Pour into pan. Bake at 350°F for 48 to 53 minutes or until toothpick inserted in center comes out clean. Cool in pan 25 minutes. Invert onto serving plate.

3. Dry fruit thoroughly between layers of paper towels. Arrange fruit pieces on top of cake. Brush with warmed preserves. Drizzle remaining preserves over top and sides of cake. Garnish with mint leaves, if desired. Serve warm or cool completely and refrigerate until ready to serve.

> **Tip:** *For a different presentation, you can brush the cake with warmed preserves and serve your favorite fruit assortment on the side.*

STICKY CARAMEL PECAN COFFEECAKE

8 servings

COFFEECAKE
1 package Duncan Hines® Bakery Style Cinnamon Swirl Muffin Mix

1 package (¼ ounce) active dry yeast
1 egg
¾ cup warm water (105° to 115°F)

TOPPING
⅔ cup firmly packed brown sugar
¼ cup butter or margarine, melted
1 tablespoon honey

2 teaspoons all-purpose flour
½ cup chopped Fisher® pecans

1. Preheat oven to 350°F.

2. **For coffeecake,** combine muffin mix, contents of topping packet from Mix and yeast in large bowl. Stir until blended. Knead swirl packet from Mix for 10 seconds. Cut off one end of swirl packet. Squeeze contents onto dry ingredients. Add egg and water. Stir until thoroughly blended. Set aside.

3. **For topping,** combine brown sugar, melted butter, honey and flour in small bowl. Stir in pecans. Spread evenly in ungreased 9-inch round cake pan. Gently spread reserved batter over topping. Bake at 350°F for 45 to 50 minutes or until toothpick inserted halfway in center comes out clean. Immediately invert onto serving plate. Serve warm or cool completely.

> **Tip:** *To reheat leftovers, place serving of coffeecake on microwave-safe plate. Microwave at HIGH (100% power) for 10 seconds or until warm.*

CRISP WAFFLES WITH FRUIT   Four 9-inch waffles

1 package Duncan Hines®
    Bakery Style Blueberry
    Muffin Mix
  Assorted fresh fruit pieces such
    as strawberry slices, pineapple
    tidbits, grape halves, peach or
    nectarine slices or raspberries
¾ cup all-purpose flour
1 teaspoon baking powder

2 eggs
1¼ cups milk
5 tablespoons butter or
    margarine, melted
  Confectioners sugar, for garnish
  Whipped cream (optional)
  Mint leaves, for garnish
    (optional)

1. Preheat and lightly grease waffle iron following manufacturer's directions.

2. Rinse blueberries from Mix with cold water and drain. Combine with assorted fresh fruit; set aside.

3. Combine muffin mix, contents of topping packet from Mix, flour and baking powder in large bowl. Break up any lumps. Add eggs, milk and melted butter. Stir until moistened, about 50 strokes. Pour one-fourth of batter onto center of grid of preheated waffle iron. Spread to edges. Close lid. Bake following manufacturer's directions or until golden brown and steaming stops. Remove baked waffle carefully with fork. Repeat with remaining batter. Dust lightly with confectioners sugar. Top with fruit mixture, whipped cream and mint leaves, if desired. Serve immediately.

Tip: *These waffles are also delicious served with warm maple or blueberry syrups.*

Crisp Waffle with Fruit

FRENCH APPLE TARTS

24 tarts

PASTRY

1 package Duncan Hines® Bakery
    Style Cinnamon Swirl
    Muffin Mix
1 cup all-purpose flour

1 package (8 ounces) cream
    cheese, softened
½ cup butter, softened

FILLING

7 cups Granny Smith apples,
    peeled and chopped
3 tablespoons butter or margarine
⅓ cup water

¼ cup sugar
2 tablespoons lemon juice
    Cinnamon swirl packet from Mix
    Crumb topping packet from Mix

1. Preheat oven to 350°F.

2. **For pastry,** combine muffin mix and flour in medium bowl. Place cream cheese and ½ cup butter in large bowl. Beat at low speed with electric mixer until blended. Add dry ingredients. Beat at low speed until combined. Shape dough into 24 (1½-inch) balls. Press each ball into bottom and up sides of 2½-inch ungreased muffin cup. Bake at 350°F for 12 to 14 minutes or until set and golden.

3. **For filling,** combine apples and 3 tablespoons butter in large saucepan. Add water, sugar, lemon juice, contents of cinnamon swirl packet from Mix and contents of crumb topping packet from Mix. Cook and stir on medium-high heat until apples are tender.

4. To assemble, fill each warm pastry shell with 2 tablespoons filling. Bake at 350°F for 15 to 20 minutes or until bubbly. Cool in pans for 5 to 10 minutes. Loosen sides with thin knife or spatula; remove from pan. Serve warm or cool completely on cooling racks.

> **Tip:** *For best flavor, serve warm topped with small scoop of ice cream or slices of cheddar cheese.*

WATERMELON SLICES

3 to 4 dozen cookies

1 package Duncan Hines® Golden
   Sugar Cookie Mix
1 egg

12 drops red food coloring
5 drops green food coloring
Chocolate sprinkles

1. Combine cookie mix, contents of buttery flavor packet from Mix and egg in large bowl. Stir until thoroughly blended; reserve ⅓ cup dough.

2. For red cookie dough, combine remaining dough with red food coloring. Stir until evenly tinted. On waxed paper, shape dough into 12-inch-long roll with one side flattened. Cover; refrigerate with flat side down until firm.

3. For green cookie dough, combine reserved ⅓ cup dough with green food coloring in small bowl. Stir until evenly tinted. Place between 2 layers of waxed paper. Roll dough into 12×4-inch rectangle. Refrigerate for 15 minutes.

4. Preheat oven to 375°F.

5. To assemble, remove green dough rectangle from refrigerator. Remove top layer of waxed paper. Trim edges along both 12-inch sides. Remove red dough log from refrigerator. Place red dough log, flattened side up, along center of green dough. Mold green dough up to edge of flattened side of red dough. Remove bottom layer of waxed paper. Trim excess green dough, if necessary.

6. Cut chilled roll with flat side down into ¼-inch-thick slices with sharp knife. Place 2 inches apart on ungreased baking sheets. Sprinkle chocolate sprinkles on red dough for seeds. Bake at 375°F for 7 minutes or until set. Cool 1 minute on baking sheets. Remove to cooling racks. Cool completely. Store between layers of waxed paper in airtight container.

Tip: *To make neat, clean slices, use unwaxed dental floss.*

Watermelon Slices

RUGELACH

48 pastries

PASTRY

1 package Duncan Hines® Bakery Style Cinnamon Swirl Muffin Mix
1 cup all-purpose flour

1 package (8 ounces) cream cheese, softened
½ cup butter, softened

FILLING

Topping packet from Mix
1½ cups finely chopped Fisher® walnuts
1 cup raisins

¼ cup granulated sugar
Cinnamon swirl packet from Mix
2 tablespoons butter, melted
Confectioners sugar (optional)

1. **For pastry,** combine muffin mix and flour in medium bowl. Place cream cheese and ½ cup butter in large bowl. Beat at low speed with electric mixer until blended. Add dry ingredients. Beat at low speed until combined. Divide dough into three equal balls. Wrap each ball in plastic wrap; refrigerate for 1 hour.

2. **For filling,** combine contents of topping packet from Mix, walnuts, raisins and granulated sugar in small bowl. Knead swirl packet from Mix for 10 seconds. Squeeze contents into nut mixture. Stir until uniform and crumbly.

3. Preheat oven to 350°F.

4. To assemble, flatten one ball on floured pastry cloth. Roll into 13-inch circle about ⅛ inch thick. Brush lightly with melted butter. Cut into 16 pie-shaped pieces. Sprinkle one-third of filling (about 1 cup) evenly over pieces. Roll up each piece starting at wide end. Place pastries on ungreased baking sheet with points on bottom. Bake at 350°F for 13 to 15 minutes or until light golden brown. Cool 1 minute on baking sheet. Remove to cooling rack. Repeat with remaining pastry and filling. Cool completely. Dust with confectioners sugar, if desired. Store in airtight container.

> **Tip:** *For ease in cutting pastry, use a pizza cutter.*

FUDGY COOKIE SQUARES

24 to 48 squares

COOKIE CRUST

1 package Duncan Hines®
  Chocolate Chip Cookie Mix

1 egg
2 teaspoons water

TOPPING

1 can (14 ounces) sweetened
  condensed milk
1 package (12 ounces) semi-sweet
  chocolate chips
2 tablespoons butter or margarine

1 cup chopped Fisher® walnuts
1 tablespoon vanilla extract
  Walnut halves, for garnish
  (optional)

1. Preheat oven to 350°F.

2. **For cookie crust,** combine cookie mix, contents of buttery flavor packet from Mix, egg and water in large bowl. Stir until thoroughly blended. Spread in ungreased 13×9×2-inch pan. Bake at 350°F for 13 to 15 minutes or until light golden brown. Cool completely.

3. **For topping,** combine sweetened condensed milk, chocolate chips and butter in medium saucepan. Cook on low heat, stirring constantly, until chips are melted. Remove from heat. Add chopped walnuts and vanilla extract; stir until blended. Spread over cookie crust. Score into squares with tip of knife. Place walnut half on top of each square, if desired. Refrigerate until firm. Cut into squares. Refrigerate until ready to serve.

> **Tip:** *Bar cookies look best when cut neatly into uniform sizes. Measure with ruler using knife to mark surface. Cut with sharp knife.*

CHOCOLATE CHIP BARS

20 to 24 bars

COOKIE BARS

1 package Duncan Hines® Moist
  Deluxe Yellow Cake Mix
  (see Tip)
¼ cup butter or margarine,
  melted
¼ cup firmly packed brown sugar

¼ cup water
2 eggs
1½ cups semi-sweet chocolate
  chips
½ cup chopped Fisher® pecans
  or walnuts

DRIZZLE

½ cup semi-sweet chocolate chips

2 teaspoons Crisco® Shortening

(continued on page 52)

Fudgy Cookie Squares

Chocolate Chip Bars, continued

1. Preheat oven to 375°F. Grease and flour 13 × 9 × 2-inch pan.

2. **For cookie bars,** combine cake mix, melted butter, brown sugar, water, eggs, 1½ cups chocolate chips and pecans in large bowl. Mix with spoon until thoroughly blended. Spread in pan. Bake at 375°F for 20 to 25 minutes or until light golden brown. Cool completely.

3. **For drizzle,** combine ½ cup chocolate chips and shortening in small microwave-safe bowl. Microwave at MEDIUM (50% power) for 1 minute; stir. Repeat until chocolate is melted. Drizzle over cooled bars. Allow chocolate to set before cutting into bars.

> **Tip:** *For **Fudgy Chocolate Chip Bars,** substitute Duncan Hines® Moist Deluxe Swiss Chocolate Cake Mix for the Yellow Cake Mix.*

EASTER EGG COOKIES   4 dozen cookies

1 package Duncan Hines® Golden Sugar Cookie Mix	**Assorted colored decors**
1 egg	**Corn syrup**
	Food coloring

1. Preheat oven to 375°F.

2. Combine cookie mix, contents of buttery flavor packet from Mix and egg in large bowl. Stir with wooden spoon until thoroughly blended.

3. Place 1 level *measuring* teaspoonful dough on ungreased baking sheet about 2 inches apart for each cookie. Flatten dough into egg shape (an oval with one narrow end and one wide end). Decorate half the eggs with assorted decors. Press lightly into cookie dough. Bake at 375°F for 6 to 7 minutes or until cookies are light golden brown around the edges. Cool 1 minute on baking sheets. Remove to cooling racks. Cool completely.

4. To decorate plain cookies, combine 1 tablespoon corn syrup and 1 or 2 drops food coloring in small bowl for each color. Stir to blend. Paint designs with tinted corn syrup using clean artist paint brushes. Sprinkle painted areas with colored decors, if desired. Store between layers of waxed paper in airtight container.

> **Tip:** *Keep cookie dough an even thickness when shaping for more even baking.*

PEANUT BUTTER
CHOCOLATE BLOSSOMS   3 dozen cookies

1 package Duncan Hines® Peanut
    Butter Cookie Mix
3 tablespoons unsweetened cocoa
1 egg
1 teaspoon grated orange peel

2½ teaspoons orange juice
    Sugar
36 milk chocolate kiss candies,
    wrappers removed

1. Preheat oven to 375°F.

2. Combine cookie mix, contents of peanut butter packet from Mix, cocoa,
egg, orange peel and orange juice in large bowl. Stir until thoroughly blended.
Shape dough into 36 (1-inch) balls. Roll in sugar. Place 2 inches apart on
ungreased baking sheets. Bake at 375°F for 10 to 12 minutes or until set.
Immediately top each cookie with chocolate kiss. Press down firmly until
cookie cracks around edges. Cool 1 minute on baking sheets. Remove to
cooling racks. Cool completely. Store in airtight container.

> **Tip:** *You may substitute milk chocolate candy stars for the
> milk chocolate kiss candies.*

CHOCOLATE MACADAMIA
COOKIES   3 dozen cookies

1 package Duncan Hines®
    Chocolate Chip Cookie Mix
¼ cup unsweetened cocoa
1 egg

1 tablespoon water
⅔ cup coarsely chopped
    macadamia nuts

1. Preheat oven to 375°F.

2. Combine cookie mix and cocoa in large bowl. Add contents of buttery
flavor packet from Mix, egg and water. Stir until thoroughly blended. Stir in
macadamia nuts. Drop by rounded teaspoonfuls 2 inches apart onto ungreased
baking sheets. Bake at 375°F for 8 to 10 minutes or until set. Cool 1 minute on
baking sheets. Remove to cooling racks. Cool completely. Store in airtight
container.

> **Tip:** *You may substitute chopped pecans or walnuts for the macadamia nuts.*

Peanut Butter Chocolate Blossoms

ELEGANT ALMOND BARS   20 large or 32 small bars

CRUST
1 package Duncan Hines® Golden
   Sugar Cookie Mix
1 egg

1 tablespoon water
½ teaspoon almond extract

FILLING
1 can (8 ounces) almond paste
¼ cup sugar
¼ cup butter or margarine, melted

2 eggs
½ cup Fisher® sliced natural
   almonds

GLAZE
2 ounces white chocolate baking
   bars, coarsely chopped
2 tablespoons Crisco® Shortening

¼ cup Fisher® sliced natural
   almonds

1. Preheat oven to 350°F.

2. **For crust,** combine cookie mix, contents of buttery flavor packet from Mix, 1 egg, water and almond extract in large bowl. Stir until thoroughly blended. Spread in ungreased 13 × 9 × 2-inch pan. Bake at 350°F for 11 to 13 minutes or until light golden brown.

3. **For filling,** combine almond paste, sugar and melted butter in large bowl. Beat at low speed with electric mixer until blended. Add 2 eggs; beat until thoroughly blended. (Batter may be slightly lumpy.) Spread over hot crust. Sprinkle with ½ cup almonds. Bake at 350°F for 19 to 21 minutes or until filling is set. (It is normal for filling to puff up while baking.) Cool completely.

4. **For glaze,** combine white chocolate and shortening in small heavy saucepan. Melt on low heat, stirring constantly until smooth. Drizzle over cooled bars. Sprinkle with ¼ cup almonds. Allow glaze to set before cutting into bars.

Tip: *Lower oven temperature by 25°F when using glass baking dishes. Glass heats more quickly and retains heat longer.*

YUMMY CHOCOLATE CHIP
FLOWER COOKIES
24 cookies

1 package Duncan Hines®
  Chocolate Chip Cookie Mix
1 egg
2 teaspoons water
24 flat ice cream sticks

1 container (16 ounces) Duncan
  Hines® Vanilla Layer Cake
  Frosting
Yellow and red food coloring
Assorted colored decors

1. Preheat oven to 375°F.

2. Combine cookie mix, contents of buttery flavor packet from Mix, egg.and
water in large bowl. Stir until thoroughly blended. Shape dough into
24 (1-inch) balls. Place 3 inches apart on ungreased baking sheets. Push ice
cream stick into center of each ball. Flatten dough slightly. Bake at 375°F for
7 to 8 minutes or until light golden brown. Cool 1 minute on baking sheets.
Remove to cooling racks. Cool completely.

3. Spoon half the Vanilla frosting into small bowl. Add 3 to 4 drops yellow
food coloring. Stir until blended. Add 3 to 4 drops red food coloring to
frosting in container. Stir until blended. Place each tinted frosting in small
resealable plastic bag; seal. Snip pinpoint hole in bottom corner of each bag.
Decorate one cookie with frostings. Sprinkle with assorted decors. Repeat
with remaining cookies.

> **Tip:** *To make a cookie bouquet, arrange cookies in a small clean clay or
> plastic flower pot filled with marbles, jelly beans or other assorted candies.
> For the finishing touch, wrap colorful ribbon around the pot
> and tie into a big bow.*

OATMEAL CARMELITAS
9 to 12 servings

1 package Duncan Hines®
  Chocolate Chip Cookie Mix
1 cup quick-cooking oats (not
  instant or old-fashioned)
1 tablespoon plus 1½ teaspoons
  water

½ cup chopped Fisher® pecans
½ cup caramel ice cream topping
1 tablespoon plus 1½ teaspoons
  all-purpose flour

(continued on page 60)

Yummy Chocolate Chip Flower Cookies

Oatmeal Carmelitas, continued

1. Preheat oven to 350°F. Grease sides of 8-inch square pan (see Tip).

2. Combine cookie mix, contents of buttery flavor packet from Mix, oats and water in large bowl. Stir until thoroughly blended. Reserve 1 cup crumb mixture. Press remaining crumb mixture into pan. Bake at 350°F for 12 to 14 minutes or until set and lightly browned. Remove from oven.

3. Sprinkle pecans over baked base. Combine ice cream topping and flour in small bowl. Stir until blended. Drizzle over pecans. Sprinkle with reserved crumb mixture. Bake 25 to 28 minutes longer or until golden brown. Loosen bars from edge of pan with knife. Cool completely. Cut into bars.

> **Tip:** *Oatmeal Carmelitas will be easier to remove from the pan if the sides have been greased.*

PEANUT BUTTER DREAMS   2½ dozen cookies

1 package Duncan Hines® Peanut Butter Cookie Mix	1 package (6 ounces) semi-sweet chocolate chips
1 egg	½ cup sweetened condensed milk
Sugar	30 Fisher® pecan halves

1. Preheat oven to 375°F.

2. Combine cookie mix, contents of peanut butter packet from Mix and egg in large bowl. Stir until thoroughly blended. Shape into 30 (1-inch) balls. Place 2 inches apart on ungreased baking sheets. Flatten with bottom of large glass dipped in sugar to make 2-inch circles. Bake at 375°F for 7 to 8 minutes or until set. Cool 1 minute on baking sheets. Remove to cooling racks. Cool completely.

3. Place chocolate chips and sweetened condensed milk in small saucepan. Cook on low heat, stirring constantly, until chips are melted. Drop 1 teaspoonful fudge mixture on top of each cookie. Top with pecan half. Repeat with remaining cookies, fudge mixture and pecan halves. Allow fudge to set before storing between layers of waxed paper in airtight container.

> **Tip:** *For evenly baked cookies, place the baking sheet in the center of the oven, not touching the sides.*

ALMOND HEARTS

4 to 5 dozen cookies

1 package Duncan Hines® Golden
   Sugar Cookie Mix
¾ cup ground Fisher® almonds
2 egg yolks
1 tablespoon water

14 ounces (6 cubes) vanilla flavored
   candy coating
   Pink candy coating, for garnish
   (optional)

1. Preheat oven to 375°F.

2. Combine cookie mix, contents of buttery flavor packet from Mix, ground almonds, egg yolks and water in large bowl. Stir until thoroughly blended.

3. Divide dough in half. Roll half the dough between 2 sheets of waxed paper into 11-inch circle. Slide onto flat baking sheet. Refrigerate about 15 minutes. Repeat with remaining dough. Loosen top sheet of waxed paper from dough. Turn over and remove second sheet of waxed paper. Cut dough with 2½-inch heart cookie cutter. Place cutouts 2 inches apart on ungreased baking sheets. (Roll leftover cookie dough to ⅛-inch thickness between sheets of waxed paper. Chill before cutting.) Repeat with remaining dough circle. Bake at 375°F for 6 to 8 minutes or until light golden brown. Cool 1 minute on baking sheets. Remove to cooling racks. Cool completely.

4. Place vanilla candy coating in 1-quart saucepan on low heat. Stir until melted and smooth. Dip half of one heart cookie into candy coating. Allow excess to drip back into pan. Place cookie on waxed paper. Repeat with remaining cookies. Place pink candy coating in small saucepan on low heat. Stir until melted and smooth. Spoon into pastry bag fitted with small writing tip. Decorate top of cookies as desired. Allow candy coating to set before storing between layers of waxed paper in airtight container.

Tip: *Cookies may be stored in airtight containers in freezer
for up to 6 months.*

Almond Hearts

CHOCOLATE PEANUT BUTTER CONFECTION

16 to 20 servings

BROWNIES
1 package Duncan Hines®
Chocolate Lovers' Double
Fudge Brownie Mix

¾ cup Fisher® peanuts

FILLING
1 package (8 ounces) cream cheese,
softened

1½ cups confectioners sugar
¾ cup Jif® Creamy Peanut Butter

TOPPING
1 package (6-serving size) vanilla
instant pudding and pie
filling mix
2½ cups milk
1 container (8 ounces) frozen
whipped topping, thawed

½ cup Fisher® peanuts
1 bar (1.55 ounces) milk chocolate,
chopped

1. Preheat oven to 350°F. Grease bottom of 13 × 9 × 2-inch pan.

2. **For brownies,** prepare brownies following package directions for basic recipe. Stir in ¾ cup peanuts. Bake and cool as directed.

3. **For filling,** place cream cheese in small bowl. Beat at medium speed with electric mixer until smooth. Add confectioners sugar; beat at low speed until smooth. Add peanut butter; beat until blended. Spread on cooled brownies.

4. **For topping,** place pudding mix and milk in large bowl. Beat at low speed for 2 minutes. Fold in whipped topping. Spread over filling. Sprinkle ½ cup peanuts evenly over pudding mixture. Gently press into topping. Sprinkle with chocolate. Refrigerate until ready to serve.

> **Tip:** *Overbaking brownies will cause them to become dry. Closely follow the recommended baking times given in recipes.*

Chocolate Peanut Butter Confection

PETER RABBIT BROWNIE

12 servings

BROWNIE

1 package Duncan Hines®
    Chocolate Lovers' Double
    Fudge Brownie Mix
2 eggs

⅓ cup water
⅓ cup Crisco® Oil or
    Crisco® Puritan® Oil

FROSTING

1 container (16 ounces) Duncan
    Hines® Vanilla Layer Cake
    Frosting, divided

Red food coloring
Assorted candies, for face
Pink pipe cleaners, for whiskers

1. Preheat oven to 350°F. Grease bottoms of two 8-inch round cake pans. Line with waxed paper.

2. **For brownie,** combine brownie mix, eggs, water and oil in large bowl. Stir with spoon until well blended, about 50 strokes. Spread evenly in pans. Bake at 350°F for 25 to 28 minutes or until set. Cool in pans 15 minutes. Remove from pans. Peel waxed paper from bottoms. Cool completely.

3. **For frosting,** tint ⅓ cup Vanilla frosting with red food coloring to desired pink color.

4. To assemble, cut one brownie layer as shown, removing 2-inch-wide slice from center. Arrange as shown. (Piece #3 is not used. Eat as a snack with ice cream.) Spread remaining Vanilla frosting on sides and top of brownie. Spread pink frosting on ears. Decorate with candies and pipe cleaners (see Photo).

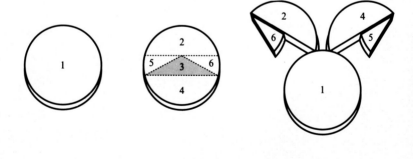

Tip: *For ease in cutting brownies, refrigerate until well chilled and use a knife with a thin, sharp blade.*

MINIATURE CHEESECAKE TEMPTATIONS

24 mini-cheesecakes

CRUST
1 package Duncan Hines®
    Chocolate Lovers' Milk
    Chocolate Chunk Brownie Mix

FILLING
3 packages (8 ounces each) cream
    cheese, softened
¾ cup sugar
2 tablespoons all-purpose flour
3 eggs, lightly beaten
2 tablespoons lemon juice

1 teaspoon vanilla extract
2 cups sweetened whipped cream,
    for garnish
Fresh strawberries, sliced,
    for garnish
Mint leaves, for garnish

1. Preheat oven to 350°F. Place 24 (2½-inch) foil liners in muffin cups.

2. **For crust,** prepare brownies following package directions for basic recipe. Divide batter evenly into foil liners. Bake at 350°F for 5 minutes.

3. **For filling,** place cream cheese in large bowl. Beat at low speed with electric mixer, adding sugar and flour gradually. Add eggs, lemon juice and vanilla extract, mixing only until incorporated. Spoon evenly over warm crusts, filling cups half full. Return to oven. Bake at 350°F for 20 minutes longer. Cool completely.

4. To serve, garnish with dollops of whipped cream, strawberry slices and mint leaves.

Tip: *You may substitute Duncan Hines® Fudge Brownie Mix, Family Size, for the Chocolate Lovers' Milk Chocolate Chunk Brownie Mix.*

TEA PARTY BROWNIE HEARTS

24 to 28 brownie hearts

1 package Duncan Hines® Fudge
    Brownie Mix, Family Size
2 eggs
⅓ cup water
⅓ cup Crisco® Oil or
    Crisco® Puritan® Oil

1 container (16 ounces) Duncan
    Hines® Vanilla Layer Cake
    Frosting
Red food coloring
Assorted decors, nonpareils or
    candies

(continued on page 70)

Miniature Cheesecake Temptations

Tea Party Brownie Hearts, continued

1. Preheat oven to 350°F. Grease bottom of 15½ × 10½ × 1-inch jelly-roll pan.

2. Combine brownie mix, eggs, water and oil in large bowl. Stir with wooden spoon until well blended, about 50 strokes. Pour into pan. Spread evenly. Bake at 350°F for 22 to 27 minutes or until brownies are set. Cool completely.

3. Place frosting in medium bowl. Add red food coloring 1 drop at a time. Stir with wooden spoon until well blended and desired color.

4. To assemble, cut brownies with heart cookie cutter. Remove hearts from pan with pancake turner. Place on serving tray. Spread pink frosting on top of one heart. Decorate with decors. Repeat for remaining brownie hearts. Allow frosting to set. Store between layers of waxed paper in airtight container.

> **Tip:** *After cutting heart shapes, there will be leftover pieces of brownies. Place them in a plastic resealable bag and freeze for a snack on another day.*

CHOCOLATE BUNNY COOKIES   4 dozen cookies

1 package Duncan Hines® Fudge Brownie Mix, Family Size	1⅓ cups Fisher® pecan halves (96)
1 egg	1 container (16 ounces) Duncan Hines® Dutch Fudge Layer Cake Frosting
¼ cup water	
¼ cup Crisco® Oil or Crisco® Puritan® Oil	Vanilla milk chips

1. Preheat oven to 350°F. Grease baking sheets.

2. Combine brownie mix, egg, water and oil in large bowl. Stir with spoon until well blended, about 50 strokes. Drop by 2 level teaspoonfuls 2 inches apart onto greased baking sheets. Place two pecan halves, flat-side up, onto each cookie for ears. Bake at 350°F for 10 to 12 minutes or until set. Cool 2 minutes on baking sheets. Remove to cooling racks. Cool completely.

3. Spread Fudge frosting on one cookie. Place vanilla milk chips, upside down, on frosting for eyes and nose. Dot each eye with Fudge frosting using toothpick. Repeat for remaining cookies. Allow frosting to set before storing between layers of waxed paper in airtight container.

> **Tip:** *For variety, frost cookies with Duncan Hines® Vanilla Frosting and use semi-sweet chocolate chips for the eyes and noses.*

Chocolate Bunny Cookies

YOGURT BROWNIES

24 brownies

1 package Duncan Hines® Fudge
   Brownie Mix, Family Size
2 egg whites

⅓ cup Dannon® Low-Fat Vanilla
   Yogurt
Confectioners sugar

1. Preheat oven to 350°F. Grease bottom of 13×9×2-inch pan.

2. Combine brownie mix, egg whites and yogurt in large bowl. Stir with spoon until well blended, about 50 strokes (batter will be thick). Spread in pan. Bake at 350°F for 22 to 24 minutes or until set. Cool completely. Cut into bars. Dust with confectioners sugar as desired.

Note: This recipe contains no cholesterol.

> **Tip:** *Dannon® Low-Fat Plain Yogurt and 1 teaspoon vanilla extract may be substituted for the Low-Fat Vanilla Yogurt.*

PEANUTTY PICNIC BROWNIES

24 brownies

1 package Duncan Hines® Fudge
   Brownie Mix, Family Size
1 cup quick-cooking oats (not
   instant or old-fashioned)
1 egg

⅓ cup water
⅓ cup Crisco® Oil or
   Crisco® Puritan® Oil
¾ cup peanut butter chips
⅓ cup chopped peanuts

1. Preheat oven to 350°F. Grease bottom of 13×9×2-inch pan.

2. Combine brownie mix, oats, egg, water and oil in large bowl. Stir with spoon until well blended, about 50 strokes. Stir in peanut butter chips. Spread in pan. Sprinkle with peanuts. Bake at 350°F for 25 to 28 minutes or until set. (Do not overbake.) Cool completely. Cut into bars.

> **Tip:** *Always use the pan size called for in Duncan Hines® recipes. Using a different size pan can give brownies an altogether different texture.*

PINEAPPLE COCONUT CHEESE TART

9 servings

1 cup flaked coconut, divided
1 package Duncan Hines® Golden Sugar Cookie Mix
1 container (16 ounces) Duncan Hines® Cream Cheese Layer Cake Frosting

1 package (8 ounces) cream cheese, softened
1 can (15¼ ounces) pineapple tidbits, drained
1 cup frozen whipped topping, thawed

1. Preheat oven to 350°F. Line bottom and sides of 9-inch round cake pan with aluminum foil (see Tip).

2. Spread ½ cup coconut evenly on baking sheet. Toast in 350°F oven for 5 to 7 minutes or until golden brown. Cool completely; set aside.

3. Combine cookie mix and contents of buttery flavor packet from Mix in large bowl. Stir until thoroughly blended. (Mixture will be crumbly.) Press evenly on bottom and ½ inch up sides of lined pan. Bake at 350°F for 14 to 16 minutes or until light golden brown. Cool completely.

4. Combine Cream Cheese frosting and cream cheese in large bowl. Beat with electric mixer at medium speed for 2 minutes or until creamy. Add remaining ½ cup untoasted coconut, pineapple and whipped topping. Stir until thoroughly blended. Pour into prepared crust. Sprinkle with toasted coconut. Refrigerate for 4 hours or until firm.

5. To serve, lift edges of aluminum foil to remove tart from pan. Remove foil carefully. Place tart on serving plate.

Tip: *For ease in lining cake pan, shape aluminum foil to fit by forming over bottom and sides of pan. Remove and place inside pan.*

Pineapple Coconut Cheese Tart

EXQUISITE BROWNIE TORTE   12 to 16 servings

FILLING
- 1 package (3 ounces) cream cheese, softened
- ⅓ cup confectioners sugar
- ¼ teaspoon almond extract
- 1 package whipped topping mix
- ½ cup milk

RASPBERRY SAUCE
- 1 tablespoon cornstarch
- 2 tablespoons cold water
- 1 package (10 ounces) frozen raspberries in light syrup, thawed
- 2 tablespoons seedless red raspberry jam
- ¼ teaspoon lemon juice
- 1 tablespoon Amaretto (optional)
- 1 package Duncan Hines® Chocolate Lovers' Walnut Brownie Mix
- ½ pint fresh raspberries
- ½ cup fresh blueberries
- Mint leaves, for garnish

1. **For filling,** combine cream cheese, confectioners sugar and almond extract in large bowl. Beat at medium speed with electric mixer until softened and blended. Add whipped topping mix and milk. Beat at high speed for 4 minutes or until mixture thickens and forms peaks. Cover. Refrigerate for 2 to 3 hours or until thoroughly chilled.

2. **For raspberry sauce,** dissolve cornstarch in water in medium saucepan. Add thawed raspberries, raspberry jam and lemon juice. Cook on medium-high heat until mixture comes to a boil. Remove from heat; add Amaretto, if desired. Push mixture through sieve into small bowl to remove seeds. Refrigerate for 2 to 3 hours or until thoroughly chilled.

3. Preheat oven to 350°F. Line 9-inch springform pan with aluminum foil. Grease bottom of foil.

4. Prepare brownies following package directions for basic recipe. Spread in pan. Bake at 350°F for 35 to 37 minutes or until set. Cool completely. Remove from pan. Peel off aluminum foil.

5. To assemble, place brownie torte on serving plate. Spread chilled filling over top of brownie. Place ¼ cup raspberry sauce in small resealable plastic bag. Snip pinpoint hole in bottom corner of bag. Drizzle sauce in three concentric rings one inch apart. Draw toothpick in straight lines from center to edge through topping and sauce to form web design. Arrange fresh raspberries and blueberries in center. Garnish with mint leaves. Serve with remaining sauce.

> **Tip:** *This is a great make-ahead recipe. Prepare the filling, sauce and brownie torte one day in advance. Assemble just before serving.*

Exquisite Brownie Torte

TRUFFLES

3 dozen candies

1 container (16 ounces) Duncan
   Hines® Milk Chocolate Layer
   Cake Frosting
2½ cups confectioners sugar
1 cup Fisher® pecan halves, divided

1 cup semi-sweet chocolate chips
3 tablespoons Crisco® Shortening
   Flaked coconut, for garnish
   (optional)

1. Combine Chocolate Frosting and confectioners sugar in large bowl. Stir
with wooden spoon until thoroughly blended.

2. Cover each of 36 pecan halves with 1 tablespoon candy mixture. Roll into
1-inch balls; set aside. Chop remaining pecans; set aside.

3. Place chocolate chips and shortening in 2-cup glass measuring cup.
Microwave at MEDIUM (50% power) for 2 minutes; stir. Microwave for
1 minute longer at MEDIUM; stir until smooth. Dip one candy ball into
chocolate mixture until completely covered. Remove with fork to cooling rack
(see Tip). Sprinkle top with chopped pecans and coconut, if desired. Repeat
with remaining candy balls. Allow to stand until chocolate mixture is set.
Store in airtight container.

Note: For peanut butter flavored coating, place 1 cup peanut butter chips and
3 tablespoons Crisco® Shortening in 2-cup glass measuring cup. Microwave at
MEDIUM (50% power) for 2 minutes; stir until smooth. Dip candy balls as
directed above.

---

*Tip: Place waxed paper under cooling rack to catch drips
and make cleanup easy.*

PEACHES 'N' CREAM
ICE CREAM CAKES

2 cakes (24 servings)

1 package Duncan Hines® Moist
   Deluxe French Vanilla
   Cake Mix
½ gallon peach ice cream, softened
2 containers (8 ounces each) frozen
   whipped topping, thawed

Fresh strawberries, for garnish
Fresh peach slices, for garnish
Mint leaves, for garnish

(continued on page 80)

Peaches 'n' Cream Ice Cream Cakes, continued

1. Preheat oven to 350°F. Grease and flour two 9-inch round cake pans.

2. Prepare, bake and cool cake following package directions for basic recipe. Freeze layers until firm.

3. Line two 9-inch round cake pans with aluminum foil. Spread half the softened ice cream evenly in each pan. Freeze until firm.

4. To assemble, place one frozen cake layer on serving plate. Spread top with thin layer of whipped topping. Remove one ice cream layer from freezer. Peel off foil. Place ice cream on cake layer. Frost sides and top with half the whipped topping. Repeat with remaining cake, ice cream layer and whipped topping. Freeze until firm. Garnish with strawberries, peach slices and mint leaves just before serving.

> **Tip:** *Allow cakes to stand at room temperature 15 minutes before serving.*

"KEAKI'S HOOMAO" (JACKIE'S DESSERT)

12 to 16 servings

1 package Duncan Hines® Angel
   Food Cake Mix
2 packages (4-serving size) vanilla
   instant pudding and pie
   filling mix
4 cups milk

1 can (20 ounces) crushed
   pineapple, drained
1 cup flaked coconut
1 cup macadamia nuts, chopped
1 container (12 ounces) frozen
   whipped topping, thawed
¼ cup toasted coconut (see Tip)

1. Preheat oven to 375°F.

2. Prepare, bake and cool cake following package directions. Trim bottom crust from cake. Tear cake into bite-size pieces. Place in ungreased 13 × 9 × 2-inch pan. Prepare pudding following package directions using 4 cups milk. Stir in pineapple as pudding begins to thicken. Pour pudding mixture over cake pieces. Sprinkle with coconut and macadamia nuts. Spread with whipped topping to cover completely. Sprinkle with toasted coconut. Refrigerate until ready to serve.

> **Tip:** *To toast coconut, spread evenly on baking sheet. Toast in 350°F oven for 3 minutes. Stir and toast 1 to 2 minutes until light brown. Cool completely.*

"Keaki's Hoomao" (Jackie's Dessert)

STRAWBERRY BANANA TART

9 servings

CRUST
  1 package Duncan Hines® Golden
    Sugar Cookie Mix

FILLING
  2 teaspoons lemon juice
  1 medium banana, sliced
  1 container (16 ounces) Duncan
    Hines® Cream Cheese Layer
    Cake Frosting
  1 package (8 ounces) cream
    cheese, softened
  1 package (10 ounces) frozen,
    sweetened sliced strawberries,
    thawed and drained

  2 cups frozen whipped topping,
    thawed and divided
    Fresh strawberries, for garnish
    Mint leaves, for garnish
    (optional)

1. Preheat oven to 350°F. Line bottom and sides of 9-inch square pan with aluminum foil.

2. **For crust,** combine cookie mix and contents of buttery flavor packet from Mix in large bowl. Stir until thoroughly blended. (Mixture will be crumbly.) Press evenly on bottom and ½ inch up sides of lined pan. Bake at 350°F for 14 to 16 minutes or until light golden brown. Cool completely.

3. **For filling,** sprinkle lemon juice over banana slices; set aside. Combine Cream Cheese frosting and cream cheese in large bowl. Beat at medium speed with electric mixer for 2 minutes or until creamy. Fold in thawed strawberries, banana slices and 1 cup whipped topping. Pour into prepared crust. Cover. Refrigerate for 4 hours or overnight.

4. To assemble, lift edges of aluminum foil to remove tart from pan. Remove foil carefully. Place tart on serving plate. Garnish with remaining whipped topping, fresh strawberries and mint leaves, if desired.

> **Tip:** *To soften cream cheese, remove foil wrapper and place on microwave-safe plate. Microwave at MEDIUM (50% power) for 1½ minutes.*

ORANGE BLOSSOM CAKE   12 to 16 servings

CAKE
1 package Duncan Hines® Moist
   Deluxe White Cake Mix
3 eggs

1¼ cups orange juice
⅓ cup Crisco® Oil or
   Crisco® Puritan® Oil

FILLING and FROSTING
1 can (14 ounces) sweetened
   condensed milk
½ cup frozen orange juice
   concentrate, thawed
½ teaspoon grated orange peel
1 container (8 ounces) frozen
   whipped topping, thawed

Orange wedges, for garnish
Orange peel, for garnish
Mint leaves, for garnish
   (optional)

1. Preheat oven to 375°F. Grease and flour two 9-inch round cake pans.

2. **For cake,** combine cake mix, eggs, orange juice and oil in large bowl. Beat at low speed with electric mixer until moistened. Beat at medium speed for 2 minutes. Divide evenly into pans. Bake and cool following package directions.

3. **For filling and frosting,** combine sweetened condensed milk, orange juice concentrate and orange peel in small bowl. Stir until blended. Cover and refrigerate until thickened.

4. To assemble, place one cake layer on serving plate. Spread with half the orange filling. Top with second cake layer. Spread remaining filling on top to within 1 inch of edge. Frost sides and remaining top edge of cake with whipped topping. Garnish with orange wedges, orange peel and mint leaves, if desired. Refrigerate until ready to serve.

Tip: *Orange blossoms are frequently associated with weddings. Arrange a few fresh blossoms around the base of the frosted cake.*

REGAL CHOCOLATE ROLLS   16 to 20 servings

CAKE
1 package Duncan Hines® Angel
    Food Cake Mix
1 cup water
¼ cup unsweetened cocoa
2 tablespoons all-purpose flour

¾ cup Crisco® Oil or
    Crisco® Puritan® Oil
3 eggs
½ teaspoon vanilla extract
    Confectioners sugar

MOUSSE
2 packages (6 ounces each) white
    baking bars, chopped
4 cups whipping cream

2 teaspoons vanilla extract
    Chocolate curls, for garnish

1. Preheat oven to 350°F. Line two 15½ × 10½ × 1-inch jelly-roll pans with aluminum foil.

2. **For cake,** combine Egg White Mixture (blue "A" packet) from Mix and water in large bowl. Blend at low speed with electric mixer for 1 minute. Beat at high speed until stiff peaks form; set aside. Combine Cake Flour Mixture (red "B" packet) from Mix, cocoa, flour, oil, eggs and ½ teaspoon vanilla extract in large bowl. Beat at low speed until blended. Beat at medium speed for 3 minutes. Fold beaten egg white mixture into chocolate batter. Divide evenly into pans. Spread evenly. Bake at 350°F for 15 minutes or until set. Invert cakes at once onto lint-free kitchen towels dusted with confectioners sugar. Remove foil carefully. Trim edges of cake. Starting at short end, roll up each cake with towel jelly-roll fashion. Cool completely.

3. **For mousse,** place chopped white baking bars and whipping cream in medium saucepan. Melt on low heat, stirring until smooth. Stir in 2 teaspoons vanilla extract. Pour into large bowl. Refrigerate 4 to 5 hours or until mixture is well chilled and thickened. Divide mousse in half. Beat each half at high speed until stiff peaks form. (Do not overbeat.)

4. To assemble, unroll cakes. Spread one-fourth of mousse to edges of one cake. Reroll and place seam-side down on serving plate. Repeat with second cake. Frost rolls with remaining mousse. Garnish with chocolate curls. Refrigerate until ready to serve.

Tip: *For best results, chill bowl and beaters before whipping mousse mixture.*

SUMMER LAYER TARTS

16 to 20 servings

CAKE
1 fresh lemon
1 package Duncan Hines® Moist
    Deluxe Lemon Supreme
    Cake Mix
1 package (4-serving size) vanilla
    instant pudding and pie
    filling mix

4 eggs
⅓ cup Crisco® Oil or
    Crisco® Puritan® Oil

TOPPING
2 cups whipping cream, chilled
2 tablespoons confectioners sugar
1 cup raspberry jelly, melted
2 pints fresh strawberries, rinsed,
    drained and sliced

1 pint fresh blueberries, rinsed
    and drained (see Tip)

1. Preheat oven to 350°F. Grease and flour two 9-inch round cake pans.

2. Grate 1 tablespoon lemon peel; set aside. Squeeze juice from lemon. Add
water to equal 1 cup liquid; set aside.

3. **For cake,** combine cake mix, pudding mix, eggs, reserved liquid, oil and
lemon peel in large bowl. Beat at low speed with electric mixer until
moistened. Beat at medium speed for 2 minutes. Divide evenly into pans.
Bake at 350°F for 28 to 31 minutes or until toothpick inserted in center comes
out clean. Cool in pan 15 minutes. Invert onto cooling rack. Cool completely.

4. **For topping,** combine whipping cream and confectioners sugar in large
bowl. Beat at high speed until stiff peaks form.

5. To assemble, place one cake layer on serving plate. Glaze with ½ cup
melted raspberry jelly. Spread with 2 cups whipped cream mixture to within
½ inch of cake edge. Arrange half the strawberry slices and blueberries on
top. Repeat for second cake. Refrigerate until ready to serve.

Tip: *If fresh blueberries are not available, frozen dry pack blueberries,
thawed, may be substituted.*

Summer Layer Tart

CHOCOLATE PETITS FOURS

24 to 32 servings

1 package Duncan Hines® Moist
   Deluxe Dark Dutch Fudge
   Cake Mix
1 package (7 ounces) pure
   almond paste

½ cup seedless red raspberry jam
3 cups semi-sweet chocolate chips
½ cup plus 1 tablespoon
   Crisco® Shortening

1. Preheat oven to 350°F. Grease and flour 13 × 9 × 2-inch pan.

2. Prepare, bake and cool cake following package directions for basic recipe. Remove from pan. Cover and store overnight (see Tip). Level top of cake. Trim ¼-inch strip of cake from all sides. (Be careful to make straight cuts.) Cut cake into small squares, rectangles or triangles with serrated knife. Cut round and heart shapes with 1½ to 2-inch cookie cutters. Split each individual cake horizontally into two layers.

3. For filling, cut almond paste in half. Roll half the paste between two sheets of waxed paper to ⅛-inch thickness. Cut into same shapes as individual cakes. Repeat with second half of paste. Warm jam in small saucepan on low heat until thin. Remove top of one cake. Spread ¼ to ½ teaspoon jam on inside of each cut surface. Place one almond paste cut-out on bottom layer. Top with second half of cake, jam-side down. Repeat with remaining cakes.

4. For glaze, place chocolate chips and shortening in 4-cup glass measuring cup. Microwave at MEDIUM (50% power) for 2 minutes; stir. Microwave for 2 minutes longer at MEDIUM; stir until smooth. Place 3 assembled cakes on cooling rack over bowl. Spoon chocolate glaze over each cake until top and sides are completely covered. Remove to waxed paper when glaze has stopped dripping. Repeat process until all cakes are covered. (Return chocolate glaze in bowl to glass measuring cup as needed; microwave at MEDIUM for 30 to 60 seconds to thin.)

5. Place remaining chocolate glaze in resealable plastic bag; seal. Place bag in bowl of hot water for several minutes. Dry with paper towel. Knead until chocolate is smooth. Snip pinpoint hole in bottom corner of bag. Drizzle or decorate top of each petit four. Let stand until chocolate is set. Store in single layer in airtight containers.

Tip: *To make cutting the cake into shapes easier, bake the cake one day before assembling.*

Chocolate Petits Fours

LUSCIOUS CARAMEL CHEESECAKE

12 to 16 servings

CRUST
1 package Duncan Hines®
   Chocolate Chip Cookie Mix

1 teaspoon water

CARAMEL LAYER
1 package (14 ounces) caramels,
   wrappers removed

1 can (5 ounces) evaporated milk
1 cup chopped Fisher® pecans

FILLING
2 packages (8 ounces each) cream
   cheese, softened
¾ cup sugar
1 teaspoon vanilla extract

3 eggs
¾ cup semi-sweet chocolate chips
1 cup sweetened whipped cream,
   for garnish

1. Preheat oven to 375°F.

2. **For crust,** combine cookie mix, contents of buttery flavor packet from Mix and water in large bowl. Stir with fork until thoroughly blended. (Mixture will be crumbly.) Press on bottom and 1 inch up sides of ungreased 9-inch springform pan. Bake at 375°F for 12 to 15 minutes or until lightly browned. *Reduce oven temperature to 350°F.*

3. **For caramel layer,** place caramels and milk in medium saucepan. Stir on medium heat until caramels are melted. Remove from heat. Stir in pecans. Cool while preparing filling.

4. **For filling,** combine cream cheese, sugar and vanilla extract in large bowl. Beat at medium speed with electric mixer until blended. Add eggs, one at a time, beating after each addition (see Tip).

5. To assemble, pour caramel mixture into baked crust. Sprinkle with chocolate chips. Pour filling over chips. Bake at 350°F for 40 to 50 minutes or until set. Loosen cake from sides of pan with knife or spatula. Cool completely on rack. Remove sides of pan. Refrigerate. Garnish with sweetened whipped cream just before serving.

> **Tip:** *Overbeating cheesecake batter can incorporate too much air, which may cause the cheesecake to crack during baking.*

Recipe Index

NOTES

Duncan Hines.

NOTES

METRIC CONVERSION CHART

VOLUME MEASUREMENT (dry)

⅛ teaspoon = .5 mL
¼ teaspoon = 1 mL
½ teaspoon = 2 mL
¾ teaspoon = 4 mL
1 teaspoon = 5 mL
1 tablespoon = 15 mL
2 tablespoons = 25 mL
¼ cup = 50 mL
⅓ cup = 75 mL
⅔ cup = 150 mL
¾ cup = 175 mL
1 cup = 250 mL
2 cups = 1 pint = 500 mL
3 cups = 750 mL
4 cups = 1 quart = 1 L

VOLUME MEASUREMENT (fluid)

1 fluid ounce (2 tablespoons) = 30 mL
4 fluid ounces (½ cup) = 125 mL
8 fluid ounces (1 cup) = 250 mL
12 fluid ounces (1½ cups) = 375 mL
16 fluid ounces (2 cups) = 500 mL

WEIGHT (MASS)

½ ounce = 15 g
1 ounce = 30 g
3 ounces = 85 g
3.75 ounces = 100 g
4 ounces = 115 g
8 ounces = 225 g
12 ounces = 340 g
16 ounces = 1 pound = 450 g

DIMENSION

1/16 inch = 2 mm
⅛ inch = 3 mm
¼ inch = 6 mm
½ inch = 1.5 cm
¾ inch = 2 cm
1 inch = 2.5 cm

OVEN TEMPERATURES

250°F = 120°C
275°F = 140°C
300°F = 150°C
325°F = 160°C
350°F = 180°C
375°F = 190°C
400°F = 200°C
425°F = 220°C
450°F = 230°C

BAKING PAN SIZES

Utensil	Inches/ Quarts	Metric Volume	Centimeters
Baking or	8×8×2	2 L	20×20 ×5
Cake pan	9×9×2	2.5 L	22×22 ×5
(square or	12×8×2	3 L	30×20 ×5
rectangular)	13×9×2	3.5 L	33×23 ×5
Loaf Pan	8×4×3	1.5 L	20×10 ×7
	9×5×3	2 L	23×13 ×7
Round Layer	8×1½	1.2 L	20×4
Cake Pan	9×1½	1.5 L	23×4
Pie Plate	8×1¼	750 mL	20×3
	9×1¼	1 L	23×3
Baking Dish	1 quart	1 L	
or	1½ quart	1.5 L	
Casserole	2 quart	2 L	